# The

# Chesapeake Bay

# Retriever

## – A Complete Anthology of the Dog –

### *1890-1940*

ISBN No.
978-14455-2583-9 (Paperback)
978-14455-2703-1 (Hardback)

**British Library Cataloguing-in-Publication Data**
A catalogue record for this book is available from
the British Library

VDB
www.vintagedogbooks.com

# Contents

Containing chapters from the following sources:

Robt. Millbank's, 154 West Forty-eighth Street, New York.
PRIDE.

## THE CHESAPEAKE BAY DOG.

ORIGIN.—Not known positively, but probably a cross between
the two Labrador dogs that swam ashore from a sinking ship in
Chesapeake Bay and the English water-spaniel.

USES.—Retrieving wild fowl from the water. There are three
classes of these dogs: the otter, tawny, sedge-colored, with very
short hair; the curly-haired and the straight-haired, each red brown;
a white spot is not unusual.

* SCALE OF POINTS, ETC.

| | | | | Value. | | | | | | Value. |
|---|---|---|---|---|---|---|---|---|---|---|
| Head | . | . | . | . 15 | Coat | . | . | . | . | . 15 |
| Neck | . | . | . | . 5 | Tail | . | . | . | . | . 5 |
| Shoulders | . | . | . | . 10 | Feet | . | . | . | . | . 10 |
| Chest | . | . | . | . 15 | Legs | . | | . | . | . 10 |
| Size | . | . | . | . 5 | | | | | | |
| Loins | . | . | . | . 10 | Total | | . | . | . 100 |

WEIGHT.—Dogs, 80 pounds; bitches, 65 pounds.

HEIGHT.—About 25 inches in dogs; 23 inches in bitches.

Measurements are as follows: from fore toe to top of back, 25 inches; tip of nose to base of head, 10 inches; girth of body, 33 inches; breast, 9 inches; around fore foot, 6 inches; around forearm below shoulder, 7 inches; between eyes, $2\frac{1}{4}$ inches; length of ears, 5 inches; from occiput to root of tail, 35 inches; tail, 16 inches long; around muzzle below eyes, 10 inches.

The Standard says nothing as to the dog's conformation. The illustration, therefore, must be the guide.

Dr. Robert Milbank's (154 West 48th St., New York City)
"KENT"

## THE CHESAPEAKE BAY DOG

**Origin.**—The origin of this breed, unfortunately, is unknown. Those who are seemingly in the best position to know all concerning it, both by research and having for many years bred it, claim that it probably owes its origin to a cross between two Labrador dogs of doubtful breeding that swam ashore from a sinking ship in the Chesapeake Bay, and an English Water Spaniel. With the Boston Terrier, this dog can properly be said to be of purely American origin.

**Uses.**—Retrieving wild fowl both from water and land, and when properly broken will retrieve equally well any of our game birds.

### *STANDARD.

**Head.**—Broad, running to nose, only a trifle pointed, but not at all sharp. Eyes of yellow color, ears small, placed well up on head, and face covered with very short hair.

**Neck.**—Only moderately long, and with a firm, strong appearance.

**Shoulders and Chest.**—Shoulders and chest should have full liberty, with plenty of show for power and no tendency to restriction of movement. Chest strong and deep.

**Back, Quarters and Stifles.**—These should show fully as much, if not more power than the fore-quarters, and be capable of standing prolonged strain. Any tendency to weakness must be avoided.

3

**Legs, Feet, etc.**—Short, showing both bone and muscle, and provided with well-webbed feet of good size ; fore-legs rather straight and symmetrical. It is to be understood that short legs do not convey the idea of a dumpy foundation. Elbows well let down, and set straight, for development of easy movement.

**Stern.**—Stout, somewhat long, the straighter the better, and showing only moderate feather.

**Coat.**—Thick and short, somewhat coarse, with tendency to wave over shoulders, back and loins, but nowhere should it be more than one and a quarter to one and a half inch in length ; that on flanks, legs and belly shorter, growing much shorter near the feet. Under all this, a short, woolly fur, which should well cover the skin, and can be observed by pressing aside the outer coat.

**Color.**—Nearly resembling wet sedge grass, though towards Spring it becomes lighter by exposure to the weather. A small white spot or frill on breast is admissable. Color is important, as the dog in most cases is apt to be outside the blind, consequently one that is too dark is objectionable, the deep liver of the spaniel making much greater contrast, is therefore to be avoided.

**Weight.**—About 65 lbs., too large a dog being unwieldy and lacking quickness of movement. Bitches usually are smaller than the dog, but not necessarily so.

**Symmetry and Quality.**—The Chesapeake Bay dog should show a bright, lively, intelligent expression, with general outline good at all points ; in fact, a dog worthy of notice in any company.

### *SCALE OF POINTS.

| | | | |
|---|---:|---|---:|
| Head, including ears, lips and eyes | 14 | Legs, elbows, hocks and feet | 14 |
| Neck | 6 | Stern | 4 |
| Shoulders and chest | 14 | Symmetry and quality | 6 |
| Back, quarters and stifles | 14 | Coat and texture | 16 |
| | | Color | 12 |

Total ................................................................. 100

### COMMENTS.

The Chesapeake Bay dog being essentially a field dog, it is but rarely seen on our benches. Right royally he performs the duties of the English retriever, a real choice specimen of which there is probably not one in the States. It is a thousand pities that this dog is not better known among our sportsmen, for there does not exist one that is brighter, gamier and withal a better companion afield. There is no sea too rough for him to buffet and retrieve his dead or crippled bird, whether it be snipe or swan, no duck too cleverly diving not to be captured, nor woodcock too deeply hidden in a swale for him not to be all afire till his work is accomplished, nor will he leave it until the desired end is attained.

As the dog is called upon to retrieve every bird, whether it be an English snipe or a Canadian goose, the weakness of jaw that is too often apparent, should be studiously avoided, the rather long jaw, if full of

4

strength, being especially desirable. Many of our most prominent breeders demand that the ears shall be wholly free of hair, as shown in the pointer, and wholly unlike the spaniel's. The standard calls for short legs, but care must be taken that they are not too much so, and if a choice has to be made between a too short or a too long-legged specimen, the latter is decidedly preferable. As the dog is often called upon to retrieve heavy birds from icy waters, the back and hind-quarters should be very powerful, and any weakness in these parts should be heavily penalized. Too small feet are by many objected to, while hair growing between the toes indicates, some claim, the incross of spaniel blood, even though it be very far removed.

The coat should be very dense, and one, that by easily using both hands in parting will cause the skin to be *plainly* visible, should be deemed most objectionable.

The setter tail, as shown in Mr. J. M. Tracy's painting of Barnum, is objected to by many breeders, the fancy leaning to one that is nearly cylindrical in shape, with closely matted hair at the root. At the other end of the dog, it should be always insisted upon that its eyes be yellow, pure and simple, all others being emphatic blemishes.

Those of our sportsmen who indulge in duck, goose or snipe shooting, will be fully alive to the value of color in a retriever, so, as it carries twelve points out of a possible one hundred, it should never be overlooked. Strength without coarseness should be sought for in every feature, nor should it be wanting in any one of them.

5

### THE CHESAPEAKE BAY DOG

NE of the few dogs developed in this country is the Chesapeake Bay dog, its name being taken, obviously, from that great ducking resort on the Atlantic coast. The dog was developed for retrieving ducks, and naturally we have a dog well fitted for the work.

There are three stories regarding the origin of this dog, one of which has to be put down as an impossibility, and from the other two the reader can take his choice or dismiss them both and conclude that a gradual process of selection of a dog fitted for the work developed the variety. The impossible story is that a retrieving bitch, in order to be kept away from the dogs, was tied up in a marsh near an otter den and subsequently had puppies which were supposed to own an otter as their sire, and from him came what is still called the otter coat. Another "tradition," as these stories were called by the late James F. Pearson, of Baltimore, is that given upon the authority of George W. Kierstead, who was also one of the acknowledged experts of twenty years ago. Mr. Kierstead claimed that the breed originated in the place of its name, and "from the best authorities obtainable, we learn that about the year 1807 the ship *Canton*, of Baltimore, Md., fell in at sea with an English brig, in a sinking condition, bound from Newfoundland to England. The crew were taken aboard the *Canton*, also two puppies, a dog and a bitch. The English crew were landed on their native soil, and the two puppies purchased from the captain for a guinea apiece and taken to Baltimore. The dog puppy, a dingy red in colour, was called Sailor, and was given to Mr. John Mercer, of West River. The bitch was black, was called Canton, and was given to Dr. James Stewart, of Sparrow Point. These dogs were compactly built— not so large as the Newfoundland; hair not long, but thick and wavy. They individually attained great reputation as duck retrievers, and it is said of them that they would follow a crippled duck for miles through ice and heavy sea, and if successful in a capture would always bring it back to their owner. The dog Sailor became the property of a gentleman of wealth, and was taken to his estate on the east shore of Maryland, where his progeny is still known as the Sailor breed.

"There is no positive proof that there were ever any dogs produced from the union of these two, Sailor and Canton, neither is there anything to show that there was no production from them. The natural supposition is that there was, and it is to these two dogs that we feel we can give credit for the now famous breed of Chesapeake Bay duck dog."

Another "tradition" is that given by Mr. Joseph A. Graham in "The Sporting Dog," in the form of a communication from General Ferdinand C. Latrobe, who has long had personal supervision of the dogs of the Carroll Island Club: "Many years ago a vessel from Newfoundland ran aground near an estate called Walnut Grove, on the shores of the Chesapeake. This estate belonged to Mr. George Law, a member of a well-known Maryland family. On board the ship were two Newfoundland dogs, which were given by the captain to Mr. Law in return for kindness and hospitality shown to himself and his crew. The beginning of the Chesapeake dog was from a cross between these Newfoundlands and the common yellow and tan coloured hound or coon dog of that part of the country.

"At the Carroll Island Club, of which the writer has been a member for over thirty years, and the records of which go back for over a century, this strain of dogs has been carefully bred, and for many years the pedigrees have been kept. The same care in breeding the Chesapeake has been followed at some of the other clubs."

General Latrobe says that the combination of the yellow and tan hound, the Newfoundland and some spaniel introductions, produced the "liver colour of the true Chesapeake Bay dog," thus placing himself apart from the other writers quoted, who all preferred the sedge colour.

As might be expected from the facts or traditions thus set forth and the mixed character of the breeding, with only the one definite aim of having the best possible retrievers, we have in the Chesapeake a dog not over burdened with good looks or quality. It will be readily seen that the standard is not an attempt to elevate or improve the breed by setting an ideal to be bred up to. What the standard describes is a plain every-day dog, with faults that would not pass muster in hardly any other breed set forth as requirements. The wedgy type of head, with the wide skull

7

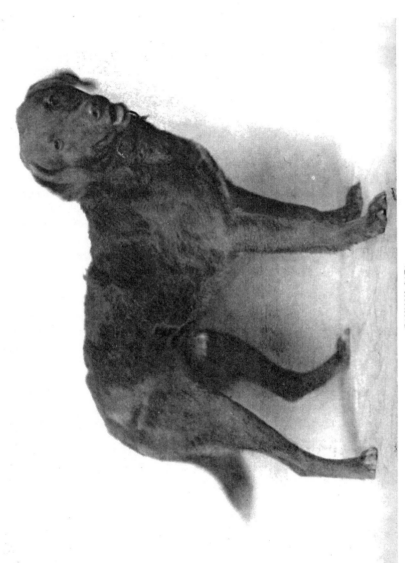

GAMMON GATA

Owned by Mr. A. M. Coghlin, Toledo, O.

8

and tapering fore face, the high-set-on ears and the short neck, the yellow eye and the long tail are not quality characteristics at all, and the gentlemen who framed the standard missed an opportunity to set a far higher mark for the dog.

If we had the making of a standard we should frame it more on the model of the description of the English retriever: The head of moderate width and good length, with a strong, well-carried-out jaw and sound teeth, evenly meeting. Eye dark hazel, and we should specify that the yellow eye is a great detraction and must be got rid of. Ears to be neat in size, set on low, and without fold. Neck of good length, and, in place of the upright shoulders which invariably accompany the short neck, we should particularly specify the sloping position of the shoulders, without which a dog cannot reach out with his feet when swimming. Then the legs should not be short for a swimming dog, and to state that the feet have to be webbed means only that they have to be ordinary feet, for all dogs' feet are webbed. It is right that they should be large. The tail or stern for such a dog should be only long enough not to look short, carried gaily in a curve, but not over the back. It should be bushy, thicker in the middle, and show no feather. With regard to the coat, our belief is in the kind that has a crisp wave in it, as it is almost sure to be dense and close, and that is what is wanted. But whether with this kink or not, the coat must be so dense that, owing to the undercoat, it cannot be parted down to the skin.

The desirable colour is a yellow liver, which goes by the name of sedge. Liver is too dark for the correct thing, though there are doubtless many good dogs nearly approaching that colour, and we do not think colour should overrule everything. We also know very well that this shade as well as the liver becomes weather bleached as it ages, and when ready to shed it is many shades lighter than the incoming coat. Sedge is most decidedly preferable, but not to the extent of knocking out a far better dog of a darker shade. We mean that we could not put an open-coated, badly made sedge dog over one good in these respects but dark in colour.

The late Mr. Pearson was a recognised authority on the breed, and in 1882 wrote to the *American Field* supporting a previous communication from a gentleman who roundly criticised the Baltimore show committee for making two classes, one being for long, curly coated dogs. That writer held that the Chesapeake was not a long-haired or curly dog, but should have a short, close coat, "without a wrinkle in it." As usual with

9

most writers upon a breed but little known, or not scientifically established—and by that we mean bred with judgment and a type in view—he said that the breed was almost entirely lost at that time. Mr. Pearson fully endorsed the first part of the letter, and on his own account wrote as follows:

"I wish clearly to lay down the rule that, according to my judgment, none other than dogs known as the otter breed or close-hair dogs should be taken as the Simon Pure of this strain. The Chesapeake Bay dog, otter breed, should be a strong, well-built animal, weighing about sixty pounds; colour much resembling wet sedge grass, though toward spring it becomes lighter from exposure to the weather. A small white spot or frill on breast is entirely admissible; a large patch of same very objectionable. Coat short and thick, with tendency to wave over shoulders, back and loins, where it is longest. Should judge hair to be nowhere more than one and a quarter inches long, and probably not over half that on flanks and legs. Head broad, nose a trifle pointed but not at all sharp, neck only moderately long; eyes of yellow colour; ears small and placed well up on the head; face covered with very short hair, and mild and intelligent in expression. Legs of moderate length, ending with feet of good size. Tail stout, somewhat long, with barely a suspicion of feather, and the straighter the better. This dog is sprightly, active, an admirable watch dog, abundantly able to take care of himself, and an admirable retriever. Females are usually smaller than the males, but not necessarily so.

"There is another style of so-called Chesapeake Bay dogs that may be mentioned; short hair, entirely straight, much darker in colour—in fact liver colour—more heavily built in every way; many of them of a surly disposition, and having a tendency to shirk their work whenever they feel so disposed, particularly in cold weather and high-running waves. I have a suspicion that they may have a touch of bloodhound through them, and from my experience do not care for anything less than a stout club when it is necessary to correct them." Mr. Pearson then briefly refers to the traditions, all of which came "through the medium of the 'oldest inhabitant,' so whatever credence is attached thereto I leave to the judgment of each reader."

Doctor Millbank, of New York, was an enthusiastic supporter of the breed up to the time of his death a few months ago, and from a communication of his in the *American Field*, of April 2, 1898, it is evident that Mr. Pearson was his mentor and guide. Acting upon the advice thus received, Doctor

A. M. COGHLIN'S CLAIRVINE

THE LATE DR. MILBANK'S PRIDE

THE LATE DR. MILBANK'S BUSH

THE LATE MR. MALLORY'S MARY

CHIEF
Owned by J. G. McPhee, Seattle

PEGGIE MAGUIRE
Owned by McFee & Gilbert, Seattle

CHESAPEAKE BAY DOGS OF MARYLAND, OHIO AND THE PACIFIC COAST

Millbank bred several generations of Chesapeakes, and was for several years the most successful exhibitor of these dogs at the New York show.

We have not much knowledge of Chesapeakes in Maryland, other than having seen such dogs as were shown at the various Baltimore shows. Some years ago there was far less uniformity in the benched specimens than has been the case of late, and we remember our old friend, Mr. Mallory, showing two dogs at a Philadelphia show which were of very different type. One was of the short, close-coated sort and the other decidedly curly. We told him we could not stand the curly as the proper type, and he fully agreed with us and said he only entered the latter to help fill the class.

When at Seattle and Portland shows in the spring of 1904 we were agreeably surprised at the number of good Chesapeakes in that section of the country. Well grown dogs with excellent coats were at both shows and the winners at Seattle were as good if not better than any dog or bitch we have seen in the East.

There is a mistaken idea that dogs such as the Chesapeake Bay dog call for expert knowledge of the breed in order to judge them. Such a claim is only true of dogs that have been specialised and improved to a high state of perfection, which is not the case with the Chesapeake, and we venture to state that those who are best acquainted with them as working dogs are not so competent to judge symmetry and an approach to quality as is an all-round judge of dogs. Give a man who is accustomed to ring work a class of Chesapeakes to judge, and all he needs to be told is what they are used for and the preferred colour. From him you will probably get far better selections than from those who may have had plenty of experience with the breed as workers but have little knowledge of dogs in general and do not possess the judging eye.

We have stated what in our opinion should be the guide for judging this breed, and it will be seen by what we give below that it differs in several essentials from what was presented to the American Kennel Club, as the work of a committee appointed in 1885 to submit a standard. The club did not adopt any of the standards so submitted, and this one remains but the expression of the opinion of Messrs. Pearson, Norris and Malcolm, who formed the committee. We believe there was a Chesapeake Bay Dog Club before that, and that this was the standard of that club, with the exception that in the scale of points each of the four properties for which a value of fifteen is given the original club figures were fourteen for each, and the four points of difference were added to colour, which made that property twelve in place of eight, as given below.

## Descriptive Particulars

*Head.*—Broad, running to nose only a trifle pointed, but not sharp; eyes of yellow colour; ears small, placed well up on head; face covered with very short hair.

*Neck.*—Should be only moderately long, and with a firm, strong appearance.

*Shoulders and Chest.*—Shoulders should have full liberty, with plenty of show for power and no tendency to restriction of movement; chest strong and deep.

*Back, Quarters and Stifles.*—Should show fully as much if not more power than fore quarters and be capable of standing prolonged strain. Any tendency of weakness must be avoided. Ducking on the broad waters of Chesapeake Bay involves, at times, facing a tide and sea, and in cases of following wounded fowl a dog is frequently subjected to a long swim.

*Legs, Elbows, Hocks and Feet.*—Legs should be short, showing both bone and muscle, and with well-webbed feet of good size; fore legs rather straight and symmetrical. It is to be understood that short legs do not convey the idea of a dumpy formation. Elbows well let down and set straight, for development of easy movement.

*Stern.*—Should be stout, somewhat long—the straighter the better—and showing only moderate feather.

*Symmetry and Quality.*—The Chesapeake Bay dog should show a bright, lively, intelligent expression, with general outlines good at all points; in fact a dog worthy of notice in any company.

*Coat and Texture.*—Short and thick, somewhat coarse, with tendency to wave over shoulders, back and loins, where it is longest; nowhere over one and a quarter to one and a half inches long; that on the flanks, legs and belly shorter, tapering to quite short near the feet. Under all this a short, woolly fur which should well cover the skin and can be readily observed by pressing aside the outer coat. This coat preserves the dog from the effects of the wet and cold, and enables him to stand severe exposure. A shake or two throws off all the water, and is conducive to speed in swimming.

A bird down. The "Bay dog" starting out to retrieve

Turning back to shore in good form

The dog, the bird, the man and the decoys—all in one picture

Bringing in the bird

The dog's share of the sport

Delivering the bird

THE CHESAPEAKE BAY DOG AT WORK

14

*Colour.*—Nearly resembling wet sedge grass, though toward spring it becomes lighter by exposure to the weather. A small spot or frill on breast is admissible. Colour is important, as the dog in most cases is apt to be outside the blind, consequently too dark is objectionable; the deep liver of the spaniel, making much deeper contrast, is to be avoided.

*Weight.*—Should be about 60 pounds, too large a dog being unwieldy and lacking quickness of movement. Bitches are usually smaller than the dogs, but not necessarily so.

### SCALE OF POINTS

| | | | |
|---|---|---|---|
| Head, including ears, lips and eyes | 15 | Stern | 4 |
| Neck | 6 | Symmetry and quality | 6 |
| Shoulders | 15 | Coat and texture | 16 |
| Back, quarters and stifles | 15 | Colour | 8 |
| Legs, elbows, hocks and feet | 15 | Total | 100 |

15

## CHESAPEAKE BAY DOGS.

THE Chesapeake Bay dog is truly an American dog. Unlike that other evolution of fancy—the Boston Terrier (*see* p. 284), a comparatively modern manufacture—the Chesapeake owes nothing to the old country. Moreover, compared to the Terrier from Boston, the Chesapeake is almost as old as the Constitution, for tradition places its birth at about the beginning of the nineteenth century. For years and years after the dogs that eventually became known as the Chesapeakes had proved their great value as duck retrievers, they were bred for use with little regard to pedigree—the best worker was the standard, consequently beauty of form was not considered. Hence, of all breeds of dogs with which our shows have made us familiar, the Chesapeake is the most lacking in refinement and type.

There are several versions as to the origin of the breed, but there would seem to be no authentic history, each duck shooting section having its pet tradition as to how the Chesapeake was evolved. One has it that in 1807 the good ship " Canton," hailing from Baltimore, Maryland, fell in with a disabled English brig bound from Newfoundland to Liverpool. The crew were taken from the brig, along with two puppies, a dog and bitch. The crew were landed in England and the two puppies were purchased for a guinea apiece, and brought to Baltimore, at that time an important city not far from the big ducking shores of the Chesapeake. The dog puppy was called Sailor, and was a dingy red, and became the property of Mr. John Mercer, of West River. The bitch was black, and named Canton, and was given to Dr. James Stewart, of Sparrow Point. These dogs are said to have been compactly built, not so large as the Newfoundland, hair thick and wavy but not long. They individually became noted as duck retrievers, and it is said of them that they would follow a wounded duck for miles through ice and heavy seas, and if successful in a capture would always bring it back to the owner. Sailor eventually became the property of a gentleman living on a large estate on the East coast of Maryland, and up to fifteen years or so ago, his descendants were known as the Sailor breed. While there is no record that Sailor and Canton were mated, nor is there any evidence to the contrary, the chances are that they were, and one faction of the lovers of the Chesapeake Bay dog insist that these two were the foundation of the present breed.

The writer has more often heard the tradition as related by Gen. Latrobe, an old Maryland sportsman, who, having had control of the ducking dogs on the preserves of the Carroll Island Club, may be credited with being familiar with his subject. According to this gentleman, many years ago a vessel from Newfoundland ran aground near an estate called Walnut Grove, on the shores of the Chesapeake. This

CHESAPEAKE BAY DOG.

estate belonged to Mr. George Law, a member of a well-known Maryland family. On board the ship were two Newfoundland dogs, which were given by the Captain to Mr. Law in return for kindness and hospitality shown to himself and crew. The General goes on to say that the beginning of the Chesapeake Bay dog was from a cross between these Newfoundlands and the common yellow and tan coloured hound or coon dog of that part of the country. To substantiate this plausible reasoning, General Latrobe, having been a member of the Carroll Island Club for thirty years, is authority that the records of the Club had been kept for over one hundred years, and that this strain of dogs has been carefully bred for many years and the pedigrees carefully preserved. The Carroll Island Club, though one of the oldest sporting clubs in the country, was not the only Maryland club which had kept a record of its Chesapeake dog breeding. General Latrobe's remark that the combination of the yellow hound, the Newfoundland and some spaniels produced the liver colour of the true Chesapeake, is in distinction to claims of other sportsmen that the true Chesapeake is sedge colour or dry rush. But this is immaterial, for we have seen them of both shades varying not at all in their general character.

Anyone who is familiar with the nondescript hounds, usually termed "coon dogs" down South, will readily concede that their mating with the sort of Newfoundland that existed a hundred years ago would produce just about such a nondescript type of dog as the Chesapeake. At the same time the Chesapeake is evidence that those who bred him knew what they were building him for. His broad skull, wedgy fore-face and strong and powerful in-jaw are necessary where a wounded duck or goose is to be retrieved from heavy seas and broken ice. Ridicule has been thrown at the high set on of ears by the purely "fancy" man, but a little reflection will show that thereby the ear is well protected in swimming. The short neck, which certainly does not make for symmetrical beauty in this dog, has also its purpose in the strength required to land a duck or goose through rush and weed and ice and waves.

Then again, one of its characteristics is a yellow eye. This we take as one of the proofs of the "coon dog" cross, and far from being out of place is usually associated with dogs of a yellow liver or sedge colour. The long tail is another point that we have seen criticised from the fancier point of view, but is not such a rudder very necessary to a dog that has to swim in the sea?

19

The coat is a most important part of the Chesapeake, for the dog must have a covering that will protect it from the icy cold waters in which it may have to swim about for hours. The Chesapeake's is a peculiar coat unlike that of all other breeds. It is coarse, thick and very dense, but lies close to the skin, and is reinforced by an undercoat that forms an impenetrable barrier to the wet and cold. This coat is in the vernacular known as the "otter coat." There are curly coated so-called Chesapeakes, but the Simon pure is the short, or comparatively short, haired sort. The proper length of coat is about one and a quarter inches long on the shoulders and half that on the legs and flank.

As a figure at American shows the breed is scarcely considered, though classes are regularly provided for them, and now and then a few turn up. They are usually consigned to the Setter judge, but it is a common saying that anyone can judge a Chesapeake. As we have pointed out the dog has been bred for use and sport alone, with no thought of fancy points, consequently it has a very homely appearance. It has a general resemblance to the English Retriever.

Sportsmen who have been identified with these dogs in the show world are Dr. Millbank, of New York, Mr. Kierstadt, Mr. Pearson, Mr. Malcolm, Mr. Mallory, and, later, Mr. Jos. Lewis, who had quite a good team of these dogs a few years ago.

A standard was made up some twenty years ago by three Marylanders, Messrs. Pearson, Norris, and Malcolm, and submitted to the American Kennel Club, and though not accepted, is still, the writer believes, the only one in existence. As will readily be seen it is somewhat vague in parts :—

### STANDARD.

*Head*—Broad, running to nose only a trifle pointed, but not sharp ; eyes of yellow colour ; ears small, placed well up on head ; face covered with very short hair. *Neck*—

20

Should be only moderately long, and with a firm, strong appearance. *Shoulders and Chest*—Shoulders should have full liberty, with plenty of show for power and no tendency to restriction of movement ; chest strong and deep. *Back, Quarters, and Stifles*—Should show fully as much if not more power than fore-quarter and be capable of standing prolonged strain. Any tendency to weakness must be avoided. Ducking on the broad waters of the Chesapeake Bay involves facing a tide and sea, and in cases of following a wounded fowl a dog is frequently subjected to a long swim. *Legs, Elbows, Hocks, and Feet*—Legs should be short showing both bone and muscle, and with well webbed feet of good size ; fore-legs rather straight and symmetrical. It is to be understood that short legs do not convey a dumpy formation. Elbows well let down and set straight for development of easy movement. *Stern*—Should be stout, somewhat long—the straighter the better—and showing only moderate feather. *Symmetry and Quality*—The Chesapeake Bay dog should show a bright, lively, intelligent expression, with general outlines good at all points ; in fact a dog worthy of notice in any company. *Coat and Texture*—Short and thick, somewhat coarse, with tendency to wave over shoulders, back and loins, where it is longest ; nowhere over one and a quarter to one and a half inches in length ; that on the flanks, legs, and belly shorter, tapering to quite near the feet. Under all this a short, woolly fur which should well cover the skin and can be readily observed by pressing aside the outer coat. The coat preserves the dog from the effects of wet and cold and enables him to stand severe exposure. A shake or two throws off all the water, and is conducive to speed in swimming. *Colour*—Nearly resembling wet sedge grass (a dull liver), though towards spring it becomes lighter owing to exposure to the weather. A small spot or frill on the breast is admissible. Colour is important, as the dog is in most cases apt to be outside the blind, consequently if too dark is objectionable ; the deep liver spaniel, making much deeper contrast, is to be avoided. *Weight*—Should be about 60 pounds, too large a dog being unwieldy and lacking in swiftness of movement. Bitches are usually smaller than the dogs but not necessarily so.

**HARRY W. LACY.**

## THE CHESAPEAKE BAY DOG

MAY be conveniently noticed at this point, since it is essentially a Retriever bred and developed for work with the gun, and mainly used on the Atlantic coast, where wild duck abound. It is one of the few breeds " invented " by our American cousins. There is a tradition that it originated from a dog or dogs rescued from a vessel bound from Newfoundland to England and wrecked on the shores of Chesapeake Bay, and that a cross with a common yellow and tan coloured hound or coon dog produced the liver or " sedge " colour of the true Chesapeake Bay Retriever. It is not a particularly handsome dog, but for its purpose it is an excellent worker. The chief characteristic which distinguishes it from a very ordinary wavy-coated English Retriever is that of colour. There is a Chesapeake Bay Dog Club with headquarters in Baltimore, whose official standard of points is as follows :—

1. **General Appearance.**—A symmetrical and well-built dog, fit for duck-shooting.
2. **Head.**—Broad, running to nose only a trifle pointed, but not at all sharp ; face covered with very short hair.
3. **Eyes.**—Of a yellow colour ; lively and intelligent in expression.
4. **Ears.**—Small, placed well on the head.
5. **Neck.**—Should be only moderately long, and with a firm, strong appearance.
6. **Shoulders.**—Should have full liberty, with plenty of show for power and no tendency to restriction of movement.
7. **Chest.**—Strong and deep.
8. **Hind Quarters.**—Should show fully as much, if not more power than the fore quarters. Any tendency to weakness must be avoided.
9. **Legs.**—Rather short, showing both bone and muscle ; fore-legs rather straight and symmetrical ; elbows well let down and set straight.
10. **Feet.**—Of good size and well webbed.
11. **Tail.**—Stout, somewhat long, the straighter the better, and showing only moderate feather.
12. **Coat.**—Short and thick, somewhat coarse, with tendency to wave over shoulders, back and loins, where it is longest, nowhere over 1¼ inches to 1½ inches long ; that on flanks, legs and belly shorter, tapering to quite short near the feet. Under all this is a short woolly fur, which should well cover the skin, and can be readily observed by pressing aside the outer coat. This coat preserves the dog from the effects of the wet and cold, and enables him to stand severe exposure and is conducive to speed in swimming.
13. **Colour.**—Nearly resembling wet sedge grass or discoloured coat of a buffalo, though toward spring it becomes lighter by exposure to weather. A small white spot or frill on the breast is admissible.
14. **Height at Shoulder.**—About 24 inches.
15. **Weight.**—Dogs from 60 lb. to 70 lb. ; bitches from 45 lb. to 55 lb.

*Photograph by C. Reid, Wishaw.*

# THE CHESAPEAKE BAY DOG

THE Chesapeake Bay Dog, or the Chesapeake Retriever, is a wonderful animal, and excels for the purpose for which he has been bred. He is presumed to be a cross between the Labrador and the otterhound, although it is possible he may have a slight percentage of other blood running through his veins.

Irrespective of breeding, he is a dog without a peer as a retriever of waterfowl; he is also a companion and a general purpose dog, and at the same time trustworthy and dependable.

The Chesapeake Bay Dog is a natural retriever, and a 100 per cent. dog, more especially where an animal is required that must stand icy water and icy winds. His coat is made up of two layers, the outer one being coarse, harsh and fairly long, the under coat being soft, close, and woolly, and water-repellent.

This breed of dog has been developed along the Atlantic seaboard, particularly in that section watered by the Chesapeake Bay. He has been bred for work, and as a utility animal stands alone.

In size the breed varies considerably. Their height at shoulders measures anything from 20 to 25 inches, and they weigh from 60 to 80 pounds. Their ears are small, set high on, giving the head a square-

CHESAPEAKE BAY

like appearance. Coats: the hair may be straight or curly, and the colour varies from straw to deep brown, with sometimes a very little white.

Although they are bred pure, they are as yet not an acknowledged breed of any of the Kennel Clubs; nevertheless, those who have the interest of the Chesapeake Bay Dogs at heart are just as particular about the way their dogs are bred as we are in this country with our popular breeds, and we can look forward to them being used in other countries before many years have passed.

THE WATER DOG OF AMERICA.
The Chesapeake dog is one of the few genuine American breeds which has also
gained a certain popularity in Canada.   It takes the place of the English retriever.

***Chesapeake Bay Dog.***—This breed is probably more buried in the soil of America than any other. In most characteristics it belongs to the type of Lesser Newfoundland. It was found in the neighbourhood of St. Johns, and there seems little reason to doubt that here really was its origin. It is almost as old as the Constitution of the States, for it is reported to go back at least to the beginning of the nineteenth century.

The Chesapeakes have long proved to be a really useful dog, somewhat on the lines of the English Retrievers. For many years they were bred for use, with little regard to pedigree, though they maintained a certain standard. It is, however, because the dog has been used very much more than shown that he has not gained in refinement.

There are many stories as to how he came to be. Perhaps the one that reads best concerns the ship *Canton* which was sailing in 1807 from Baltimore in Maryland when it fell in with a disabled English brig which was on its way from Newfoundland to Liverpool. In rescuing the brig's crew, two puppies, a dog and a bitch, were taken on board. The dog puppy was called "Sailor", was a dingy red and became the property of a Mr. John Mercer, of West River. The bitch was black, named "Canton" and was given to Dr. James Stuart, of Sparrow Point. Being in the neighbourhood of Baltimore, which was not far from the big ducking shores of Chesapeake Bay, where the dogs flourished and grew in numbers, they were called after the locality

Their retriever qualities made them much sought after by the hunters. So keen were the dogs that heavy seas and even ice did not daunt them from following a wounded duck for miles.

There are other versions of this story of their origin, and one related by General Latrobe, an old Maryland sportsman, may have much truth in it because he was genuinely interested in, and very knowledgeable about, ducking dogs. According to him, many years ago a Newfoundland vessel was stranded on the shores of Chesapeake Bay. On board the ship were two Newfoundland dogs, which were given by the captain to a Mr. George Law, who showed great kindness and hospitality to the shipwrecked crew. The General asserts that these Newfoundlands were crossed with a common yellow-and-tan coloured hound or "Coon" dog, which inhabited that part of the country, and that the Chesapeake Bay Dog was the result. Whatever the actual beginnings were, it is certain that the Carroll Island Club kept the pedigrees of the

Chesapeake Bay Dog for over a hundred years There is this also that substantiates in a measure General Latrobe's story : the wet sedge colour of the dog suggests that there may be something of the yellow hound in its composition.

There are those who give support to this theory by a half-cynical admission that the nondescript hounds known as the "Coon" dog down South would produce an unfinished type of dog such as the Chesapeake. It certainly does lack finish, but those who bred him were thoroughly aware of the purpose for which they were breeding him. He contains just the qualities necessary to fulfil his job. His broad skull, his wedgy fore-face, and his powerful jaw make him ideal, if not unique, to face heavy seas and broken ice in the pursuit of duck or goose.

There are those, too, who ridicule the high set of the ears, but here again they are fitted for the dog's job. He may not be symmetrical in the shortness of his neck, but there is certainly strength, and that is what is

*Photo]* A GOOD WORKING TYPE. *[Wide World*
'Bing", the winner of the Derby Stake, is an excellent example of the modern Chesapeake. He is a fine water and marshland worker.

required in a dog that has to carry a big bird probably through rush and reed, as well as water

The yellow eye is another "proof" of the "Coon" dog cross, while the Chesapeake also carries a long tail, often criticized by the fancier, but which is most serviceable as a rudder to the dog in the water.

One of the first essentials of the Chesapeake is his coat. He must have a covering that will protect him from the cold, for when out with the guns he will swim in the icy water for hours. Perhaps no other dog has just such a coat ; it is very dense, and, despite its coarseness, it is

THE CHESAPEAKE

The Chesapeake Bay Dog is somewhat like the Labrador Retriever, but the American dog is said to be sturdier and works under harder conditions. Often he will swim for hours in icy-cold water, retrieving.

30

reinforced close to the skin by an under-coat that
affords a most efficient protection. There are
curly-coated dogs that are known as Chesapeakes,
but it is the comparatively short-haired dog that is
truest to type. The hair should not exceed an
inch and a half in length.

For show purposes, a small white spot on the
breast is allowed, but no other white ; and it is also
permitted that a slight thickening tendency can

DUCKING.
It is important, more especially when wild fowling, to have a dog so well trained and so accustomed to the business that he will sit
quite still at the moment when the duck heave into range.  This Cheaspeake dog knows his job.

appear over the shoulders. As a matter of fact,
however, it is not much of a show dog. In Britain
it is unknown, and even in its native country,
though often classes are arranged for it, there is a
very poor entry. The numbers, indeed, are so
scanty that more often than not the Chesapeakes
find themselves consigned to the Setter judge.

But this does not matter to the man who owns
a Chesapeake. In the vast majority of cases the
dog is not wanted for looks but for work, and from
this angle an owner has seldom a complaint to
make.

31

# THE FIRST GENTLEMAN IN AMERICA

The Chesapeake Bay Dog—An Individual and an Aristocrat—
The Romance of his Beginnings—Points to look for.

I FIRST MET HIM KNEE-DEEP in water on my own fen in the wilds of Cambridgeshire. He gave me a most independent stare without the courtesy of a nod, and went on with his shooting. I was hurt but interested. He was obviously a foreigner, but I guessed from that gruff air of independence that there was a touch of British blood somewhere. So I asked his companion, one of my partners in the shoot, where the old boy came from and who he was.

"Good Lord, he's not old—he's a youngster! He's an American, the only pure-bred one in the whole country. In fact, he claims the longest and most authentic pedigree in the whole of the United States. What's more, he is the first one of his family ever to come to England."

"I could have sworn there was English blood in him somewhere," I answered. "What is he, then— Red Indian?"

"No, just pure-bred American, real native stock evolved and bred on the spot. Here, Bruce!" He whistled up the pure-bred American.

That was my first introduction to the Chesapeake Bay dog, the dog which Americans claim to be the finest water dog in the world, just naturally bred by Providence to make wildfowlers happy. But when they claim that he is pure-bred American I have my biological doubts. Listen to Mr Anthony A. Bliss, president of the American Chesapeake Club. This is what Mr Bliss says:

" The Chesapeake Bay retriever is a pure American dog. Only the Boston bull-terrier can claim with the Chesapeake the United States as its origin, and no other sporting dog has ever been developed in this country. Beyond this I do not believe that the Chesapeake has ever been imported into another country, and I am almost sure that none has ever been taken to England." Since Mr Bliss said that several Chesapeakes have come to England. They have even poked their noses into Cruft's Show. And they have made a few friends and a great many admirers.

The Chesapeake is not the sort of dog to make friends easily. He is an exclusive, almost an esoteric, person. Like all people of discrimination, he makes few friends and has lots of acquaintances. But, again being a person of discrimination, he sets a wide gulf between friends and acquaintances. I am sure he gets more fun out of life that way.

He is one of the most individual dogs I have ever known. Each dog, indeed, is an individual, and responds to particular and individual treatment. He decides in his own mind who is his master, and that is the only man he will work for. The mere fact that you own a Chesapeake does not by any means imply that you are the Chesapeake's master or that he will work for you. He is the person who decides that, and his decision depends on you—but you don't *make* the decision. Like all people of real character, there is nothing either showy or stylish about him, but he is faithful to a degree, highly sensible, a magnificent guardian, a companion without equal, and the greatest man that ever walked into a child's nursery. Any child that is at all a likeable child, fit to make friends with dogs, will at once agree with you on that point.

The odd thing about the Chesapeake is that you always think of him, quite instinctively, as " a grand old dog." That is precisely what I felt about my friend Mr Nigel Holder's seven-months-old Chesapeake, when I found him plugging through the water on his own on my fen in Cambridgeshire. He struck me as being slightly rude in his stand-offish way, but obviously a person to know, to admire, and, later on, to like. That applies to all Chesapeakes.

Their impression of power is remarkable. They give one the feeling of immense reserves of energy, of great reservoirs of knowledge, of tolerance of disposition, obstinacy of purpose, and tenacity of principle. They are responsive, and they have a lot of quiet good sense. It will take many generations of stupid women in Bayswater and *suède*-footed young men in Kensington to ruin the character of this eminently sensible working dog. He has all the dignity, the native aristocracy, the quiet good sense, and the instinctive judgment of human nature of the British working man. Foreigners can never understand that it is because of those qualities that revolutions happen in this country with, to them, such distressing infrequency.

THE 'JELLY DOGS'

The opening meet of the Guildford and Shere beagles, who hunt a large country in Surrey, and are one of the most popular packs with London followers.

*Photo Sport and General*

35

DR HELEN INGLEBY'S CHESAPEAKE BAY RETRIEVER

A grand upstanding example of a breed which is rapidly gaining in popularity.

*Photo Sport and General*

36

It is just the same with the Chesapeake. If you have two or three Chesapeakes in the kennel there will never be any disturbances in your shooting routine— none of that hoity-toity flightiness of the Gordon setter, the kiss-me-quick slobberings of the spaniel or the mental whimperings of the golden retriever. Do not imagine for a moment that I dislike any of these three excellent breeds of sporting dogs. But I mourn for individuals among them. The show-bench and the drawing-room have made fools of them, undermined their character, ruined their stamina, set their nerves on edge, reduced them from working dogs to park paddlers, tea-table sycophants, and drawing-room druggets. I doubt if you could ever do that with the Chesapeake. He will probably bite some one finally, just as a protest, and then walk out of the house, a dog in search of a man for a master.

They say that there are none of them which are highly strung—that is, none that have been brought up from a healthy puppyhood. I should like to believe that. I have met a few, and so far every one has borne out every claim made for it by its proud possessor.

How did this paragon evolve? What were its original parents, and of what crosses is it compounded in order to justify the claim that it is a native American dog?

The Chesapeake, like Venus Anadyomene, was born of the sea. It was in 1807 that an English brig went to pieces on the rocks off the coast of Maryland. The American ship *Canton* stood inshore as near as she dared, lowered her boats, and rescued the crew and the cargo, including a pair of Newfoundland puppies. The bitch was named after the rescuing ship, while the dog was appropriately christened "Sailor." When the crew were landed a number of settlers owning houses and plantations on the coast gave them hospitality and shelter. In return the crew presented them with the Newfoundland puppies. These were very soon found by the local sportsmen to be wonderful retrievers. We are told that the dog was a dingy red and that the bitch was black, both being of a much shorter-leg type than the present-day Newfoundland. A lot of nondescript dogs in the neighbourhood were bred to the pair, but there is no record of whether Sailor and Canton were ever actually mated. Queer out-crosses were produced, and the present upholders of the Chesapeake claim that the breed derives from one of these out-crosses, in which flat-coated dogs played a governing part. More detailed information on these obscure beginnings of a pedigree are being sought most carefully at the present time by the American Chesapeake Club.

By 1885 the present type had largely evolved, the main differences being that the breed then possessed one colour only, a dark brown shading into a reddish sedge. The dead-grass colour was quite unknown. The heads were more wedge-shaped, and the coats were even thicker and longer than you find in the best specimens to-day. The dog was particularly noted as being the favourite animal in use among the wild-fowlers of Chesapeake Bay, and its hardihood and strength in the rough, cold waters of that bitter coast became famous.

Just before the War shooting men in the Western states took a great fancy to the Chesapeake. Hence the dead-grass colour which was evolved to suit the Mid-Western stubble fields. The dog became smaller, its colour lighter, and, many maintain, its stamina less. The East did not tamper with colour, but they did increase the size of their dog. For a time it seemed as though there would be a wide and unbridged gulf between the two varieties, but, fortunately, since the War the breeders of the East and West have very sensibly resolved to reduce their two extremes to something more nearly appropriate to a uniform type.

The result is that the Chesapeake to-day is settling down gradually but surely into a very fine, reliable, likeable type of gun dog, full of intelligence, absolutely trustworthy, and something of which the United States has every reason to be proud. Lest I should be thought harsh in my previous remarks on the disposition of the show-bench to ruin almost any dog, let me quote the American Chesapeake Club on their ambitions for the future: " Our primary purpose is to promote field trials to such an extent as for ever to prevent bench shows from fashioning and spoiling the Chesapeake Bay retriever."

Here are the standard points of the breed as adopted by the American Chesapeake Club on the 1st of July, 1933, and approved by the American Kennel Club on the 12th of September of the same year. They are worth giving, since I hope that this excellent breed will become popular in this country—popular, that is, among real sportsmen who require real dogs, and not among show-bench exhibitors who require a tailor's dummy among dogs. First of all for the general disqualifications. They are:

1. Black or liver-coloured.
2. White on any part of body, except breast, belly, or spots on feet.
3. Feathering on tail or legs over 1¾ inches long.
4. Dew-claws, under-shot, over-shot, or any deformity.
5. Coat curly or tendency to curl all over body.
6. Specimens unworthy or lacking in breed characteristics.

Here is the general description and standard of points officially approved and drawn up, which should be noted in conjunction with the disqualifications:

*Head.* Skull broad and round with medium stop, nose medium, short muzzle pointed but not sharp. Lips thin, not pendulous. Ears small, set well up on head, hanging loosely, and of medium leather. Eyes medium large, very clear, of yellowish colour, and wide apart.

*Neck.* Of medium length, with a strong, muscular appearance, tapering to shoulders.

*Shoulders, Chest, and Body.* Shoulders sloping, and should have full liberty of action with plenty of power without any restrictions of movement. Chest strong, deep, and wide. Barrel round and deep. Body of medium length, neither dobby nor roached, but rather approaching hollowness, flanks well tucked up.

*Back Quarters and Stifles.* Back quarters should be as

high as, or a trifle higher than, the shoulders. They should show fully as much power as the forequarters. There should be no tendency to weakness in either forequarters or hindquarters. Hindquarters should be especially powerful to supply the driving power for swimming. Back should be short, well coupled, and powerful. Good hindquarters are essential.

*Legs, Elbows, Hocks, and Feet.* Legs should be medium length and straight, showing good bone muscle, with well-webbed hare feet of good size; the toes well rounded and close pasterns slightly bent, and both pasterns and hocks medium length. The straighter the legs the better.

*Stern.* Tail should be medium length—varying from: males, 12 inches to 15 inches; females, 11 inches to 14 inches; medium heavy at base, moderate feathering on stern and tail permissible.

*Coat and Texture.* Coat should be thick and short, nowhere over $1\frac{1}{2}$ inches long, with a dense, fine, woolly under-coat. Hair on face and legs should be very short and straight, with tendency to curl not permissible.

*Colour.* Any colour varying from a dark brown to a faded tan or dead-grass. Dead-grass takes in any shade of dead-grass, varying from a tan to a dull straw colour. White spot on breast and toes permissible, but the smaller the spot the better, solid colour being preferred.

*Weight.* Males, 65 to 75 lb.; females, 55 to 65 lb.

*Height.* Males, 23 inches to 26 inches; females, 21 inches to 24 inches.

*Symmetry and Quality.* The Chesapeake dog should show a bright and happy disposition and an intelligent expression, with general outlines impressive and denoting a good worker. The dog should be well proportioned, a dog with a good coat and well balanced in other points being preferable to the dog excelling in some but weak in others.

The texture of the dog's coat is very important, as the dog is used for hunting in all sorts of adverse weather conditions, often working in ice and snow. The oil in the harsh outer coat and woolly under-coat is of extreme value in preventing the cold water from reaching the dog's skin, and aids in quick drying. A Chesapeake's coat should resist the water in the same way that a duck's feathers do. When he leaves the water and shakes himself his coat should not hold the water at all, being merely moist.

Colour and coat are extremely important, as the dog is used for duck-hunting. The colour must be as nearly that of his surroundings as possible, and with the fact that dogs are exposed to all kinds of weather, often working in ice and snow, the colour and texture must be given every consideration when judging.

Courage, willingness to work, alertness, nose, intelligence, love of water, general quality, and, most of all, disposition should be given first consideration in the selection and breeding of the Chesapeake Bay dog.

| Positive Scale of Points | Points |
|---|---|
| Head, including lips, ears, and eyes | 16 |
| Neck | 4 |
| Shoulders and body | 12 |
| Back quarters and stifles | 12 |
| Elbows, legs, and feet | 12 |
| Colour | 4 |
| Stern and tail | 10 |
| Coat and texture | 18 |
| General conformation | 12 |
| Total | 100 |

42

*Note.* The question of coat and general type of balance takes precedence over any scoring table which could be drawn up.

|  | Inches |
|---|---|
| Length, head, nose to occiput | $9\frac{1}{2}$ to 10 |
| Girth at ears | 20 ,, 21 |
| Muzzle below eyes | 10 ,, $10\frac{1}{2}$ |
| Length of ears | $4\frac{1}{2}$ ,, 5 |
| Width between eyes | $2\frac{1}{2}$ ,, $2\frac{3}{4}$ |
| Girth, neck, close to shoulder | 20 ,, 22 |
| Girth of chest to elbows | 35 ,, 36 |
| Girth at flank | 24 ,, 25 |
| Length from occiput to tail base | 34 ,, 35 |
| Girth forearms at shoulders | 10 ,, $10\frac{1}{2}$ |
| Girth upper thigh | 19 ,, 20 |
| From root to root of ear, over skull | 5 ,, 6 |
| Occiput to top shoulder-blades | 9 ,, $9\frac{1}{2}$ |
| From elbow to elbow over shoulders | 25 ,, 26 |

*Explanatory Notes (Not Official).* Hocks should be well let down, with a moderate bend to stifle. Straight or cow-hocked hind-legs are a fault. Dark brown or dead-grass colours are equally preferable. A sound mover is essential.

CPSIA information can be obtained at www.ICGtesting.com
Printed in the USA
BVOW031111231212

308964BV00001B/32/P